HEADWATERS

Headwaters

ROWAN WILLIAMS

THE PERPETUA PRESS

OXFORD

First published in 2008

The Perpetua Press
26 Norham Road, Oxford OX2 6SF

Designed and typeset in Sabon by Ron Costley
Printed in Great Britain by
Oxuniprint, Oxford University Press

ISBN 1–870–882–19–9

For Gwyneth Lewis

Contents

SHAKESPEARE IN LOVE: TEN PROSPECTS

TRANSLATIONS

HEADWATERS

Invocation: a sculpture for winter

Monasterio di Bose, Northern Italy, January 2003

Landscape in pale concrete: the abstract downs,
hillocks and gullies, only adjusting slowly
into twin faces staring, cranium to cranium,
at the dove-grey, eagerly bending sky.

The first cold sting falls hours before dawn
out of the heavy miles of cloud, stirred
to an answer by the face seen only
from so far, only at night, and when

The cold has folded up the colours, shut down
wind and growing, and the rustle, crack and damp
of the short day. Sounds come sideways
like landscape at earth level, but then

They're put out for the night; we don't
have anything to go on but the sensed
profile alongside, whose eyes we can't see.
Into the fast-approaching heavy heaven

We look, guessing what open mouth brings down
the random, uninhibited and unrepeatable
designs that will pile up in these gulfs,
guessing why what we can't see draws the lick and kiss

To our strange neighbour's skull.

Death Row, Luzeera Jail

What do they spell, the fairy lights
draping the yard outside the cells?
A daily Christmas? Unwrapping the surprises
before dawn? Another day isn't, for everyone,
something to take for granted. But by the time
the sun is up, what is there left
but sitting in the litter? The new Rolex
tells you tomorrow is already planned
(and not by you). Now wake the elders,
who have ten years seniority or twenty here
in this cramped living room; but they
won't help. They have their fill of presents.
They wink back, knowingly, from time to time
at all the little glass bulbs that won't grow
into flowers. But still: on Christmas night
all Christians sing. Guests are received with smiles
and reassured: don't worry, it isn't news
that's welcome here. You needn't tell us
anything but what we know, what the lights spell:
a guest as always, as already, here
as the damp ammoniac floor.

Luzeera Jail is the main prison in Kampala; when I visited it,
some of those in the condemned section had been there for up
to twenty-three years.

Martyrs' Memorial, Namugongo

The rushes by the water
We gather every day...

So, patiently, the long reeds are laid,
smoothed, dried and rolled in homely sheaves
and stacked across the beams, too high (you hope)
for sparks. Remains of light poke a splinter
here and there through into the moving eye, but this
is a skill too practised and domestic for mistakes.

So too, like a tall reed, each young neighbour,
shaking the drops of an alien river off his skin,
is gathered, wrapped in the homely thatch,
stacked carefully, sparked into a protective blaze
whose oiled smoke builds a skilful roof
over the panic and the piled drugged anger

That beats the earth, the drums, behind the king's
long curtains. Plaited fumes weave patiently
across a bare sky, and the rain keeps off,
the splinter of the sun probes and is blunted,
rolled in the tight black thatch with the needling
sounds they will make as the smoke canopy builds
    steeply.

Burned men, after a while, make sounds like birds,
almost too high to hear. The roof's pitch.
When the smoke has cleared, the bare light

enquires, Are you safe now? Whose house is this?
Your skill has burned your home. And the bird cries
from the bare sky say, Yes, you will live here now.
    Yes, every day.

Namugongo is the site of the burning alive of some of the first
Christian converts in Uganda in 1886 at the order of King
Mwanga.

Sarov, August 2003: the Outer Hermitage

The riverbed, between the road
and the railway line is dry
in summer;

Soft sand, like air or water
welcomes and at once forgets
your step.

Eyes closed, you could be walking
shallow dunes, walking the edge
of ocean;

Open your eyes, go on across
the bridge, under the peeling birch
and pine.

The swaying leaves and needles
spin light from shafts, crests,
faces, hands,

As if, under the sea, you looked up
into the lightning, into the firing
circuits above,

Where the crisp waves are catching
the sun's wild leap from plane
to plane.

The forest fingers the summer sky,
a child's stubby arm from the pram
waving

In search of nose and lips and breast,
feeling; not knowing; recognising;
feeling

Being seen. The leaping and the firing,
learning your way round a face against
the sky.

At night, Serafim knelt on the same rock
three years long, walked from the sand
into the sea,

And drowned, night after night,
when the sun did not dance,
or the trees

Caress, and like a bear he rubbed
and nuzzled into the dark, blind
and appalled

And hungry, until the rock began
to smell of honey. Quickly he made
for the surface,

Breathed, was blinded again by the first
dry lined leaf falling from the birch,
the first

Dry lined face falling from the forgotten
worlds of sand and hurt, of death
and shining drought.

In the barrel of your lungs,
Father, the hammer swung for the first
leaping blow

Of Paschal Matins, fingers closing
like a child's on the found flesh.
My joy. My joy.

See note on page 71

The Night Kitchen: Dreamwork

1. Drawing the Curtains

The stage set beckons, a crooked street where dark
    falls,
and the windows angle, wall-eyed, from each other; my
    face
handed aslant, mirror to mirror, my voice in ricochet,
re-dressed: a low-budget chorus, recycled, rethreaded,
breathlessly changing costumes in the wings.

Cords break: too much to hold. Curtain. No curtain
    calls,
and afterwards the deep muffled seats, the velvet
    pillows,
where, with the lights up suddenly, nothing stirs.
I turn my head. You never meet another soul
in these parts. The scattered things

Under the stalls or by the exits are what got dropped
last time. Time after time I buy my ticket,
hungry, erect, shaking, to see what happens when
I dress up as my enemies or God or Mum and Dad,
touching the spiny small things daylight doesn't let me
    see

That lodge, casual, in nails and skin. When the day has
    stopped,
lights out, the real work starts; listening for cavities

inside the walls, squinting after the freezing grief
   trapped in between
those doubled glassy wings, straining to catch
myself saying a stranger's shattering words to me.

2.   Gallery: Impressionists

All through the day, the currents whisk up
sluggish pigments, tiny crests, inverted
whirlpools that end with a glossy wet flick
into bottomless air. As turbulence
drops with the sun, I close my eyes
and back away, don't open them until
my back's against the wall. And there
they are, those sticky twirls of oil,
sucked by the roving vacuums of the mind
in tousled protest, there they are, composed
in lakes and lilies, harvests, triumphant tympanums,
foggy implacable rivers under the window.

3.   Incubus

In your light, said someone,
we shall see light; and in my dark,
dark? Digging, silent, uninterrupted,

Through the strata, why stop? I know
the next one or the next is terror.
the next is always terror.

I am what I cannot bear. Why stop?
I know the face below the face below
the face is what I cannot push off, push out, bear.

4. The Place

Yes; but also the place that has been
waiting. When the corner is turned,
there is a slope down to the bay,
in heavy shadow.

Waiting. There is a low house
of sharp stones with rugs inside
and little cold windows to sit in
looking at the grass.

Waiting. There is a beach where you walk
up to your ankles in the water, wavering
on the pebbles, out to the headland,
round the last corner.

Waiting. The morning sea that says,
All streets lead here, and this is where
it isn't any longer your face that hides
waiting.

This too is the night's business.

Emmaus

First the sun, then the shadow,
so that I screw my eyes to see
my friend's face, and its lines seem
different, and the voice shakes in the hot air.
Out of the rising white dust, feet
tread a shape, and, out of step,
another flat sound, stamped between voice
and ears, dancing in the gaps, and dodging
where words and feet do not fall.

When our eyes meet, I see bewilderment
(like mine); we cannot learn
the rhythm we are asked to walk,
and what we hear is not each other.
Between us is filled up, the silence
is filled up, lines of our hands
and faces pushed into shape
by the solid stranger, and the static
breaks up our waves like dropped stones.

So it is necessary to carry him with us,
cupped between hands and profiles,
so that the table is filled up, and as
the food is set and the first wine splashes,
a solid thumb and finger tear the thunderous
grey bread. Now it is cold, even indoors,
and the light falls sharply on our bones;
the rain breathes out hard, dust blackens,
and our released voices shine with water.

Epiphany, Taliaris *

Wind smoothes the wet trees earthwards,
loud. In here, breath comes
slow. Same air; same what?

Flat leaves, a starry floor. Which
is the one that stands
still over a birth?

Sudden movement: leaf or bird?
For a moment, damp
soil escapes in light.

* Carmarthenshire, former home of the Gwynne family

Matthäuspassion: Sea Pictures

1. *Kommt Ihr Töchter*

Wind lurches down, pushing the thick sea like blankets,
scraping its breath on wood that rocks to sunken
pulses, and we are out of sight, over the other side,
cords trailing, slipping into travel: the hills under the sun
have shrunk, corners and sharp shoulders soften into
    grey
without horizon, where the wind's wet palm caresses

Dangerously. Between night and day, between light;
the fleshless hand slaps each cheek suddenly
in turn, the questions come in cold skilled voices.
Who? Where? The answers have been left behind,
in the fields under the sun, and the stir of wet grass,
the morning smell, *der Bräutigam* mounting.

Birdcries in level steps climb up the sky,
an icy stave, they say this voyage will be *with injury
and much loss.* Swell, cloud and ice, fire
running on the masts, the knowledge no one mentions
of bleached sightless wounded things
surfacing, water streaming down their awakened flanks.

2. *Erbarme dich*

Look into ice. Force the wet fingers
squeaking against the surface, sliding up into
the little interrogatives of some tiny

animal. And the glass silence holds, your face
is held, floating against the dark, the backwards
world we shall never get behind.

We never get behind the dumb denying stillness.
Not I, not I; and the glass says, Just so,
not I, and when you look into the mirror,
you know a lifetime's words can add up to
no more than this, Not I. The soundless stranger
in the dark looks back, blank and protesting

That I shall never come to him unless
I break, push down into the water and the quiet
while light melts round the string-tight horizon
and the small cries fold inside my floating skull, and I
embrace, wide-eyed, the spinning depths
slowly, white cheeks puckering and soaked.

3. *Gebt mir meinen Jesum wieder*

There are islands where we do not land.
We thread our way into the winter archipelago,
the empty shining castles, turrets and alleys,
and hope we shall avoid the rock on which, naked,
red hair frozen to the ice, he sings
as the current heaves him towards a final north.

Nothing to say but loss, he is his own
storm on a flat sea, words fast, blood slow,
and on his island's shore there is nowhere
to anchor, nobody to visit. He flings his words
at us like coins grown dull and smooth
from being clenched in sweating hands day after day.

We ease away, crossing ourselves, our faces
flaming abruptly as we begin to search
our pockets, empty them over the side; with pure
sharp little sounds, coins bounce over the floes
and waddle down the freezing midnight water. What
must we pay to get out of jail? says the gabbling fiddle.

4. *Wir setzen uns*

Back to the headland fogs, exhausted
with new grief, old treacheries, the view without
prospect,
rain falling in a slow afternoon, between light
and dark, no questions any more; the long grey
leaving of the day that never reaches night; the turning
water that will never carry us to the pole of sleep.

White nights; *wir setzen uns* in some unwelcoming
    chair
to wait. Scored down the sky, the neighing
of a car alarm, night's horses running sluggishly,
and then the unquiet of the muffled room as it bobs
on a frustrated tide that never breathes out, never
jolts into the wooden warmth of dock.

Wood, pulsing unevenly with a tired surge
as the fire fades; five o'clock cloud and damp,
clogging the throat. Slowly the line is drawn
again, tight between sea and sky, though not
where we remember, settled after the night's
fast-running sweats. With the dawn, sleep soft.

See note on page 71

Resurrection: Borgo San Sepolcro

Today it is time. Warm enough, finally,
to ease the lids apart, the wax lips of a breaking bud
defeated by the steady push, hour after hour,
opening to show wet and dark, a tongue exploring,
an eye shrinking against the dawn. Light
like a fishing line draws its catch straight up,
then slackens for a second. The flat foot drops,
the shoulders sag. Here is the world again, well-known,
the dawn greeted in snoring dreams of a familiar
winter everyone prefers. So the black eyes
fixed half-open, start to search, ravenous,
imperative, they look for pits, for hollows where
their flood can be decanted, look
for rooms ready for commandeering, ready
to be defeated by the push, the green implacable
rising. So he pauses, gathering the strength
in his flat foot, as the perspective buckles under him,
and the dreamers lean dangerously inwards. Contained,
exhausted, hungry, death running off his limbs like
    drops
from a shower, gathering himself. We wait,
paralysed as if in dreams, for his spring.

Piero della Francesca's *Resurrection* hangs in
the civic hall of Borgo San Sepolcro, Tuscany.

Carol

Frost scratching at the door,
blood has spilled across the floor;
soldiers step down the hill,
weapons fixed for the kill.

    Where is this? When?
    Here. Again.

Light cuts across the floor,
blades of wind slam back the door;
pray the child stays still,
tighten at the sudden chill.

    Where is this? When?
    Here. Again.

Past the dismantled door:
dust and linen on the floor.
He has left for the midnight hill,
to hold the troubled planets still.

    Where is this? When?
    Always. Again.

First Love on the Wall

Pouring, a steep grey snake, over the contours,
a shield, a skin, the little horns
that stand up, blinking, for surveillance
every few miles; silence; wind.

Northward are the moors, the forests,
wolves, stags and haunted lochs,
the naked folk with messages
carved on their skins.

Behind, the long roads into sun,
vines and boats, the metal wheels
and locks of victorious argument,
the common tongue, the taxes.

And now the talkative scarred skins
are here, the woods and water;
when I turn round, the Latin diagrams
and vines have vanished.

New messages rub up against the wall,
graffiti cut by walking woods
embracing, scratching, painting, wetting
the grey horned hide.

No road backward, now, only north,
to the sun in the dark loch,
the wine in the barbarian tongue,
the duty-free economy,

The common frontier, skin to skin.
The towers look blankly up and down,
nothing behind, only dead languages;
not even room here for the wind between.

Peckett Stone Woods

Fir-sifted, the wind is thin,
cautious, but its nudge
still bends the wood. Crack.

No answer to the knocking.
The wooden gong folds
down again, work done.

The woods near Trellech, Monmouthshire

Senses

Touching

The first task: to find
a frontier. I am not,
after all, everything.

Hearing

Inside, hollowness; what is
comes to me as a blow, but
not a wound.

Seeing

A million arrows, I
the target, where the lines meet
and are knotted.

Tasting

The strip of red flesh
lies still, absorbs, silent; speaks
to all the body.

Smelling

Not only servicing the lungs, the air
is woven, full
of needles.

* * *

Each door from the room says,
This is not all. Your hands will find
in the dark.

In Memory of Dorothy Nimmo

Louche tongue and steady eyes and crisp
rejoicing teeth, she settles in the grass,
presenting breathlessly a penfull of bewildered sounds,
smartly pursued and nipped, fenced but still heaving
to a boil. This is no ordinary trial: you need
to chase the flesheaters, not just the browsers,
to hold the wolf and lamb in one fold
for one long minute. A short triumph for the bruised
lungs, but the prize is not in doubt. She holds
the eyes hard, a friend (if not man's best) still.

See note on page 71

For Inna Lisnianskaya

Barefoot, down the long woodland corridors of frost,
over the needles, walks the forgotten
mistress of the king. She smells of grapes,
candles, black furs, of cooking smells
and smoke in a cramped flat. She will disturb
the clinical forest air with haze
and trembling. In the shining kingdom,
in the rich winter malls, she opens for business
with a stall of odds and ends, cheap and irregular,
and scented with a lost indoors. *Don't beg,*
she says, *from the rich, only the poor;*
get absolution from the sinner, not the saint.

See note on page 71

Alone at Last

The room is booked for me, my mother,
my last four girlfriends, me at eighteen months,
my anima, you when I met you, myself
at sticky sixteen, you as I want you, you,
you in my ambiguous dreams, me as you want me,
me as I think you want me, your father,
you at seventeen after opening night, the boy
you spent it with, Darcy and Rochester,
the man you made up at fourteen with your friends,
giggling, God and my favourite cousin. Quite a few
more have said they'd like to be there, but
there's Health and Safety to think about, after all.
What if I shouted, 'Fire', to see who runs?
Or maybe just your name, over and over,
until it sounded stupid, but brought us,
muttering excuse me, spilling things, treading
on toes, into a space the size of sixpence, the size
of an eyeball, just big enough to hear
each other breathe? Love is, I suppose
the word that has to wait till then,
if ever, till the sixpenny width of breath overheard.

The Rood of Chester
(after Gruffydd ap Meredudd)

Cut from the flowering tree,
the body sails by night
over a scouring sea,
stained red and white.

Monday at dawn, between the walls and the sand,
they saw the carpenter's masterpiece, delivered
out of the winter country on crowned waves.
The clouds' siege lifted and the rain sailed home.

Polished as bone, the oak comes through the storm
alive, fingered and pressed by winter after winter,
rolled on the gulls' table till it swims clear
between the walls and the sand at dawn.

They climbed down from the walls to see
the winter's carpentry, the skills of a far-off land
where they speak only the gulls' tongue; they walked
the noisy strand, one eye still on the white waves.,

One eye on the wind's knives. What else has winter
to deliver? The oak is spread like wings,
an eagle five times speared as it drops
out of winter between the walls and the sand.

From Adam's sandy grave
blossoms the magic rod,
stacked in the Temple's nave
to wait for the nails of God.

There is no gift like this for a city,
no wood but this for the roof, the bloodied wings,
the salted timber. They hauled it from the sand
and wrapped and hung it in the dense rafters, singing.

And like that other image form the shore,
at night its belly cracked and the men began
to scramble out, the men folded
into the eagle's wing, the men and women devoured

By its five hungry wounds. It has gathered
all who have left their walls, who were lost in winter,
on whom the towns have closed their doors;
they will make the foursquare City of the Legions

A camp of little fires for the homeless
where they sing unfamiliar songs in the gulls' tongue –
until the legions douse the hearths and take the ground
    again
and carve the oak into a whipping block for bad boys.

      When the children weep
      at their corrected fault
      the clipped bird stirs in sleep
      tasting remembered salt.

See note on page 72

Headwaters

A knife's indentation in dough, wavering
across the moor, the blunt-nosed banks,
the grey and yellow and the polished stem
twining down, spreading on a plate to warm,
gather and melt another path. Listen ahead:
crusts stiffening, voice deepening, and the cuts
reckless, the long negotiation over rubble,
sounding like the disturbing, crystal,
unreachable voices that upset your dreams,
the language you will never follow, composed
by your sleeping self. All hanging on the bright cleft
between the swelling unbaked moss, up there,
the fold into the secret, the unreachable science
flowing raw from the cut earth on its back.

Seamouth

Push push, it says, the midwife to a foreign
uncomprehending girl who hasn't even
worked out she's pregnant yet. And
Wash, it says, slapping the stained rocks
tearfully. And sometimes, Rush;
the pouring sand says it is too late,
you have forgotten where you should have been,
Brush, it demands, hand over
the tools for picturing and colouring
and tidying; they are not allowed. Hush. Hush.
Nothing you say is heard down here
as the moon's cords twist and pull
and the spray flies up; as the rock drops
and explodes in sparks, in glowing ash.

'Blind Pianist', by Evan Walters

Here is the left hand feeling, excavating
for the supports (the left hand
that in the East makes love and can't be used
to eat), the left that fingers origin and dawn, the sudden
opening lip across the darkness where day starts
building; the left hand cupping itself around
the bass's foetal curl, delving inside the coils
for the shell's echo, hoarse and damp. The left hand
runs up and down the pillars, a hand of strings
and hammers, a cat's cradle of drawn veins;
this is the hand that reads at night,
that touches base.

See note on page 72

Nave

1

Blown in their shadows on the glass screen,
the gulls invade, the sun projects them,
heavy scraps moulting from some looped black curtain,
the sudden darkness flickering; it makes you
shake your head, praying the brain is not yet
interrupted, that the thick industrial murmur
of our circuits and processions won't after all
attract the dropping wing of what may not
(so we suspect) be nearly as light as it looks.

2

Feather or paper, on its way down the deceptive
verticals, what are the choked gullies that it has
to navigate, the overcrowded passages, packed
with breath, words and draught? And still, feeling its
　　way
along the crooked shafts and hollows of dead sounds,
there is no other destination for it but here, in the space
between our feet, still restless, shifting with every
breath, but caught, never able again, now it is here,
now it has managed the stubborn air, to leave.

Western Avenue

They always looked to me then like faces:
the square hat and the long sad barred eyes
and the tall teeth of downstairs windows, grimacing
in the hopeless well-swept everlasting
afternoon, the tundra spaces, drifts
of hours piling like newspapers in the corner.

And so the furniture is recognizable, the glue
for the construction kit and last week's *Eagle*,
abstract designs on the formica table,
patterns from the electric fire on the ceiling
through an asthmatic night, the gable
raised in surprise over a stunned window.

Somewhere in the first decade, a world assembles,
sad eyes, fixed teeth, the grey moorland inside
littered with glacial debris. The flat faces still tease,
recalling how the pieces stuck together,
on the table's edge, how the lungs would seize,
while the houses were dealt out like cards for ever.

Low Light

Black with the afternoon sun behind,
the branches steadily walk upwards, a trail of
    ideograms,
while the sun lifts its own long brush, breathing out
from the field's edge, whitening the earthward surfaces.

Turn from the winter glare to the bald, tall
barley sugar twists that stretch and yawn,
and the sun's brush insists they are green,
a rising blush under the drab bedroom skin.

The sun has turned the world upside down,
blowing the snow from soil to settle under boughs,
decanting the grass essence upwards through bark
    funnels:
it shakes the cold globe before it breathes in again and
    sleeps.

Never wasting a word . . .

Never ransacking the tins piled
in the bunker for the final war, so that
we shan't find ourselves silent in the dark?

Never producing the tough plastic mass
that won't biodegrade and can't be used again,
squatting triumphantly under the squawking gulls?

Never leaving visible on the plate
the stuff that you can't swallow, stuff
they'd be grateful for in hungry somewhere else?

Never spending scarce cash on the unnecessary,
unswallowable, unrecyclable, unprocessable
once only offer? Or what?

Cockcrow

Dark and cheerless is the morn
Unaccompanied by thee.
Joyless is the day's return
Till thy mercy's beams I see.

CHARLES WESLEY

I

As if light's arrival
were a brick splintering windows;
as if it were
bones poking in the gullet,
pushing it out of shape, so that
the retching cry falls
from the beak in a cascade
of fractures, rubble, shredded flesh;
as if day's return
were a running knot against the throat.

2

Suburban children never hear it; so
the sound belongs for me with weekend
mornings in the valley; my aunt's bedroom
with the striped curtains, looking straight
towards Bethania across the road. Saturday,
empty hours and unfamiliar second cousins
dropping in. The puzzle as the slow day starts,
why does the sun rise to what sounds –

to the child's suburban ear – as if
the flesh were crying with a predator's sudden
   dig?

3

Bring the two bits of wire unsteadily
together, and the light crows
broken and sharp between them; today
and yesterday and before
are shakily joined up, the jagged
current of words or pictures
jumps back to flickering life, convulsing
the cold channels, telling me
I've used up another cistern of supplies, so
the light blinks and flutters that bit more.

4

And waking is to swallow
yesterday's broken glass;
to try to digest the bones
of words lying still
in farmyard dust, to hear
the rasp of cord running
down towards the neck:
how else should we greet
the predator that is
our shadow choking us?

5

Or, cold and confused, we never noticed
the darkness thinning out, the fire turning pale,

the faces losing warmth, the bones
showing, the waterlogged flesh; so when
the sun's eye catches, it is the shock
of a noose thrown from behind. Down
on our knees we go, grasping the hemp
so tight the bones poke through, as if
this were the rope let down from mercy's beams
to lift us raucously into the fresh splintered air.

SHAKESPEARE IN LOVE: TEN PROSPECTS

I   *Romeo and Juliet*

Drunk in the dark, they toss the shiny loops
of silk back and forth, tottering around the pinnacles.
They trip and giggle over the tiles, they dare and shout
as the web crosses, spike to starry spike, and they
do not quite see, drunk in the dark, the little knots
twining around their feet. Tongues slur, eyes cloud,
limbs become heavy; the dream clings,
a wet cloth, over faces. So, when it gets light,
there is a web draping the Gothic spears,
damp, streaked with blood and silver, fading
as it warms. And the words caught in its circles
fall to the grass like fractured stone, like crumbs
from broken towers, tiles from the roof,
leaving the attics cold, the windows streaming.

2   *A Midsummer Night's Dream*

As it gets light, the dogs sniff the wet scent,
and everyone stares, blinking, at an unfamiliar face.
All through the night, we have been chasing someone
who didn't look like that, we have been
mouthing and grunting strangers' names; now
we must find how to talk into the prose
of daylight, how to explain last night's words, the blind
desperate explosions in the forest, the long dark paths,
the tunnels where your hands feel fur and bone;
now it is time for moulding fingers on flesh rising
wet in the dawn, plaiting the shelters of shared gestures,
the eye's spark, the lip's twitch, the reminding
touch on the arm, the private smiling code, now
serious games begin, when magic has gone back to bed.

3 *Twelfth Night*

Such a long journey. Will all the shipwrecks
and the stealthy night-time break-ins, the false beards,
borrowed tights, songs with the words you can't
  remember,
money for toys, dropped rings, corsets and swords
pay for the one epiphany? Kneeling in the straw
they all cry, What you can see and hear is not
the truth; I need to tell you, all you need to know is that
I never found the words. You can be drunk
with booze, bereavement, righteousness,
until your tongue swells so that you cannot even speak
your name. M.O.A.I. Cracked and dismembered,
letters drop in the path, not to be read, the gold
and frankincense are thrown away, the eyes look
somewhere else. A cold coming, raining every day.

4 *Much Ado About Nothing*

Home from the front in time for cocktails; as if
among the balloons and fancy dress, death, terror,
betrayal retire gracefully to a back room, where they
play amicable dominoes till the carriages are called for.
No, not so easy; the disinherited chauffeurs shift and
     complain,
and drift, bored, one by one, into the party, switching
masks, voices, privacies. And the clear streams
and clever ripples catch and tear. All the prince's
     horses,
and all his men, will labour, pulling the wound
or stitching it.
 Words that were once the flashing cards
covering the table fall in drumbeats; heavily, heavily:
paper cuts can kill. Under the game's scattered tiles,
     the words
scratched on the wood read: Lose. Lose if you want
to live before the telegram arrives: Back to the front.

5   *Measure for Measure*

Only the middle of the road is paved; on one side
the whores, towering in wooden pattens, navigate
mud and night-soil; on the other, the sisters
and the friars walk barefoot, with the stink
under their soles. The paving stones fragment,
thin out, disappear, and the loud voices from each side
close in. From each side the damp waste spreads,
and joyfully the friars and whores pile trick on trick,
because this is a game where you must break
the rules to win. Alone, in the middle, standing,
tearless and pale, the two survivors, who
want shame, silence, sleep, justice, nakedness.
They look from side to side at the excited solvers
of problems. Remind us. Who found out the remedy?

Smoke, powder-scented warmth, the long haze of the
    indoor
Toulouse-Lautrec late afternoon, the lipstick on the
    cups
and well-thumbed glasses; what you don't expect to
    find here
is purity. Because this isn't going anywhere, this
isn't furthering the general good, this isn't even making
people happy. Locked in the hazy lounge, they only
    want
to play and argue. All around the awed spectators ask,
How can we scale the Alpine heights of pointless joy
    under
the afternoon clouds, where the call to come home
    never penetrates?
Don't worry. Wait. The silver bullet that will break
the cups, mirrors and ashtrays is being forged out of
that other purity, forged for the reasonable man who
    is not
hurried by his blood, who knows by instinct just
the one gesture with his thumb to turn the raging
    current off.

7 A Winter's Tale

The white cells flower in the bloodstream, images
of her, the dream of someone else's bed;
morsel by morsel she too is eaten up,
cancered and cancelled. Under the ground she goes,
and he is left, dreaming in fever of the empty beds.
There was a man dwelt by a churchyard, dwelt
in the neighbourhood of children's leprous gravestones,
boys and girls dead in the great frost. One day there is
an idiot fairground music; spring working loose.
Women return to see the king's waste land, the dry
    beds,
and the blood flows again, fresh as cut grass, the white
    cells
colour, a dead boy stands up silent, a lost girl
sees her strange parents for the first time, stones
move from monuments. Pins and needles. Life,
    unconsoled.

8   *Othello*

I was made so as to listen: a white cloth
drifting, caught for a moment on the spines
and green of this or that man's great tumbling
story, made to wipe sweat and blood earned elsewhere,
spread for the imprint of a face: Veronica's
veil, but it is not someone else's death
that stains the handkerchief handed, man-to-man,
pricked, blotched and coloured, thrown down,
pulled between fists. Now I must listen to them
slapping my story down like cards, man-to-man,
until the table is pushed over, the white cloths
drawn, the last grace said. And I can see from here
the crumpled napkin stuffed in the mouth, silencing,
as my dead mouth absolves: Nobody: I myself.

9　Macbeth

The muscles twitch, the skin crawls, all night long:
try again. Try to sleep, try to discover
the last orgasm that will take you into quiet,
the muffling of the itching mind. And each
new thrust will only coil and hone the nerves,
the lockjawed fluttering wakefulness. Be innocent
he says, of the knowledge, dearest chuck, withdrawing
slowly into an empty nursery. He sees her
playing with the dead child. She must be fed
with silences, tilts of the head, averted eyes.
Between them, through the itchy darkness,
move the unspoken things. As they drive desperately
at knifepoint into each other, they will never say
what each sees in the empty room over the other's
    shoulder.

It does not keep you safe; it does not
give you the words you need, it does not
tell you how much to pay, how much
they owe you. It will not work, like egg-yolks,
to cool the numb heat of lost eyes and treacheries.
It does not surrender to the reasonable
case for not risking everything to keep
secrets and rivals, the white line in the tickling
membrane of freedom. It will not keep you dry: rain,
like crying, sinks down to the bone.
It will not stop: not when you sleep, not
when you wake, not when you want it to,
not when you want to settle with the mirror
of your shame. Never. It will not. Never.

TRANSLATIONS

Sin

Take off the business suit, the old-school tie,
The gown, the cap, drop the reviews, awards,
Certificates, stand naked in your sty,
A little carnivore, clothed in dried turds.
The snot that slowly fills our passages
Seeps up from hollows where the dead beasts lie;
Dumb stamping dances spell our messages,
We only know what makes our arrows fly.
Lost in the wood, we sometimes glimpse the sky
Between the branches, and the words drop down
We cannot hear, the alien voices high
And hard, singing salvation, grace, life, dawn.
Like wolves, we lift our snouts: Blood, blood, we cry,
The blood that bought us so we need not die.

(From the Welsh of D. Gwenallt Jones) *See note on page 72*

Lent

A train steams into
the long tunnel. Windows up and latched,
doors checked against the rush,
the nightfall of soft smuts.

Dark, soot, smoke –
this is our luggage to carry under the single fading
    lightbulb,

pale ash on the tongue, sacking
over the fuel (flesh and soul).

A hard tunnel, narrow
for our crowding lusts, but there is nothing
for the soul's fingers to lay hold of
unless all is let go.

Out we shoot now
into a white expanse, lighting faces that have forgotten
hope. Westwards, the horizon colours:
over the hills' cranium, a red Christ sinking.

Three days' silence, dark,
the jolting seats, every hour endless.
So what shall we say, amazed, when the dead sun
turns inside out for morning?

(From the Welsh of D.Gwenallt Jones)

Christmas Eve

Who says we've got to suffer
with the thorn's splinters gouging,
when there is such a star, and such
a scent, roses and donkeys?

Who makes the stars shine so,
glowing like roses in the dawn?
Who warms the frosty night to be
a sable fur round the king's shoulders?

Here in the stable, no befores and afters:
just the heart's wild excess and the wisps of straw.
What in the end binds us to one other? The cross?
No. The child's birthcord.

(From the Russian of Inna Lisnianskaya)

Music

I'm on this diet; only someone's really keen to do
the eating and drinking for me:
a savage music, drawn from the winter's day
and the flat peat marshes.

Shamelessly greedy, it's just not the kind of guest
you take with you to dances:
it's going to squeal like a fishwifely house-elf
and break the crockery.

The waiters bring its cocktail, wine and broken glass,
a whistle for its lips, so that it can
let out its high-voltage scream, an icicle
sharp down the wires.

It fuses all the lights, crunching away as if
with mouthfuls of croutons and nuts.
It sounds like the ice-crust breaking on the marsh.
It sounds inside me.

(From the Russian of Inna Lisnianskaya)

For Akhmatova

This is where treason and forgetfulness
mingle, like conscience and disgrace.
But she arrives, the Simple, the Arrogant,
to shake me out of bed each morning.

And I'm all over her with questions:
where is there now for us to go, and why?
Why do we gather scorching roses,
weaving them into scourges for our breasts?

No, this is no self-conscious women's thing,
it's not some Shi'ite flagellation ritual –
only why, why do the words we venerate and love
set us, day after day, on fire?

(From the Russian of Inna Lisnianskaya)

For Tsvetaeva

Your bed has given up its load now you have gone;
and you can't take your time there any longer.
While we're still here, there's time enough to think
about our lives. For geniuses are born to offer dignity
to nobodies; while nobodies are born to reprimand the
    geniuses.

(From the Russian of Inna Lisnianskaya)

From the Fourth Floor

My look-out is the mountain peak of the fourth floor;
the eyes are flooded with desert, a seascape
with Bedouin tents blowing full-sail across it,
a mackerel sky, layers of quivering sea-foam.
We came here once together.

The sun has set. A stark white outline tells us
yellow moonrise is on its way, because
the sun and moon don't get divided here;
but you and I do; here's my soul
making a detour of a thousand miles

Round through the Moscow blizzard, where your
    wheels stuck fast
for good. You left your stick for me, to use it for
a compass needle, and I followed your direction
straight away. Off for a month or so to Bible lands, and
    never
letting my gaze wander from the sands and their
    remembering.

Dates blaze in clusters on the palmtrees, eucalyptus
scratches its side against the thorny aloe, and a voice
has been, all day today, crying in the wilderness,
sounding just like that creaking lift in Moscow: just the
    two
of us, a kiss exchanged as we went up.

Climbing to this fourth floor peak is hard work. But

the desert keeps going up into the sky for ever, you
    can't tell
camels' humps from clouds up there. And like a car
slipping into its garage, the pine casket slips into this
    landscape.
The real view's your death; my life is the mirage.

(From the Russian of Inna Lisnianskaya)

At the Jaffa Gate

Yes, my old king, my Solomon: still here,
your Shunemite. I can see your muscles have dried up –
not your eyes, though, sharp as ever, stripping the veils
    from all
you see. Can you strip my veils from me, as you survey
the grassy slopes, the rose-tinted vineyards, full of
    identical old crones?

You wouldn't know me now, not even naked. My
    belly's corrugated sheets
of sand. My legs used to bend like green moist twigs;
    not now.
My breast's the crumpled date left on a dried-up palm,
my veins trace patterns through my skin, clear as
    dragonflies' wings.
I wait for you sometimes, you know, by the Jaffa Gate.

Never come near you, though. Why bother my lord the
    king?
Beauty is what is exciting in women, mind in men. So
    waiting,

after years of post-coital cooling-off, I'm hot again
suddenly. It was the songs turned me on, not just the
    hard flesh –
and the one song, of course, that stripped naked love
    itself...

My God, you roused me – through my ears, my head...
and my hair, you said, looked like the sun's curling
    locks.
Any fool of a herdsman can screw without spirit, but
    it's not
how you get the blood bubbling like water on the boil,
it's breath to make the heart fly up, ripe dust from the
    peach blossom.

What you said to me I sucked and nuzzled, a bee in
    pollen.
How could it be, my Solomon, my old king, that the
    song –
the one that no one found till you – came back in your
    old age,
simpering and cheap, and made you vain, an empty
    stranger,
flat on your face to some imported golden calf?

I turn away from you, praying each day and night
for you. With love. The evening settles quietly, and I
light seven candles for you, stick them in a tray of sand,
rip my old shift and scatter ashes from the stove
on my grey hair. God save the king, I say. God damn
    the golden calf.

(From the Russian of Inna Lisnianskaya)

Notes

Sarov, August 2003: the Outer Hermitage

Serafim of Sarov is one of the most popular of Russian saints (he died in 1833). He spent a long period of isolation in the forests after many years in his monastery, to emerge as a counsellor and wonder-worker who greeted his visitors as 'My joy', and whose physical transfiguration was reported by a close associate in a narrative that has become classical in Russian spiritual writing . The site of his hermitage, and the outcrop of rock on which he prayed in his solitude, can be seen near Sarov; throughout the Soviet era and beyond, the city housed a centre for nuclear research and was a restricted area.

Matthäuspassion: Sea Pictures

The sequence around Bach's *St Matthew Passion* use the titles of various items in the work – the opening chorus, the arias describing the repentance of Peter and of Judas, the final ensemble.

In Memory of Dorothy Nimmo

Dorothy Nimmo was born in 1932, began publishing poetry in 1984 and died in 2001.

For Inna Lisnianskaya

Inna Lisnianskaya was born in what is now Azerbaijan in 1928 and began writing poetry in her twenties. She was published only in the late sixties, since when her reputation has grown steadily. She has been compared – understandably – to Anna Akhmatova, and her tribute to Akhmatova is translated in this volume. I am greatly indebted to Professor Daniel Weissbort for introducing me to Lisnianskaya's work and to his translations in *Far from Sodom*, Arc Visible Poets no.14, Arc Publications, Todmorden, 2005 (with an introduction by Elaine Feinstein), though I have not invariably followed his readings of the Russian.

The Rood of Chester

Gruffydd ap Maredudd composed his long poem (210 lines) on the 'Rood of Chester' in the third quarter of the fourteenth century. It celebrates one of the foremost pilgrimage shrines of the Welsh border in the Middle Ages, and makes use of the legend that the great cross in St John's Church in Chester had been discovered cast up on the shore of the Dee estuary. He links this with the mythical history of the True Cross, made from the tree which grew out of Adam's grave (in fact from the seed dropped into his mouth), which had also furnished wood for Solomon's Temple. According to one tradition, the Chester Rood, torn down and hacked to pieces at the Reformation, provided a whipping block for boys in the grammar school before being burned. The poem is one of the greatest masterpieces of mediaeval Welsh verse, replete with allusions not only to the Bible and the apocryphal tradition but also to Welsh legend and literary culture. It is printed with a full translation in Barry J. Lewis, *Welsh Poetry and English Pilgrimage: Gruffudd ap Maredudd and the Rood of Chester*, University of Wales Centre for Advanced Welsh and Celtic Studies Research Paper 23, Aberystwyth 2005. The present poem might be described as a variation on the themes and images of Gruffudd's work.

'Blind Pianist', by Evan Walters

Evan Walters (1893–1951) was one of the leading artists of early twentieth-century Wales, remembered for his vivid portrayals of local scenes and personalities of the Swansea Valley and elsewhere.

Sin

David Gwenallt Jones (1899–1968) was a massively influential presence in Welsh literary and intellectual life, as influential and iconic in his way as Waldo Williams and Saunders Lewis. The two poems translated here represent early and late work, reflecting the relative formality of his earliest poetry and the much looser, almost conversational, style of his last collections.